Come to the Party
with
Jesus

AN ACTION RHYME BOOK

Come to the Party with
Jesus

Leena Lane and Chris Saunderson

Beckon with hands

Let's go! Let's go!
Let's go to a party!
Come to the party, with Jesus!

Toot! Toot!
I can hear horns!
The party is starting, says Jesus.

Cup hand round ear to listen

Yum! Yum!
Just look at the food.
Let's sit at the feast, with Jesus.

Rub tummy and lick lips

Pour a drink into a pretend cup

Pour! Pour!

They're pouring a drink.

They're pouring a drink for Jesus.

Look! Look!
The wine has run out.
No wine at the party with Jesus.

Shake head and gesture with hands

Go! Go!
Help them, says Mary –
Mary, the mother of Jesus.

Stretch out hands in front

Wait! Wait!
It's not time yet.
'God has a plan,' says Jesus.

Tap wrist as though tapping a watch

Count! Count!
Let's count those jars.
Let's count those jars with Jesus.

Point and count 1, 2, 3, 4, 5, 6.

Water! Water!
Get water to fill them.
Get water to fill them, says Jesus.

Pretend to pour water into the jars

Splosh! Splosh!
The jars are full.
The jars are ready for Jesus.

Make a sploshy noise

Carry! Carry!
A drink for the master.
New wine for the master, from Jesus.

Make hands flat like a tray

Clap hands and shout hurray

Hurray! Hurray!
The party goes on.
Let's join in the party, with Jesus!

Published in the UK by Scripture Union

207-209 Queensway, Bletchley, Milton Keynes, Bucks, MK2 2EB

ISBN 1 84427 120 X

First edition 2005

Editorial Director Annette Reynolds

Art Director Gerald Rogers

Pre-production Krystyna Hewitt

Production John Laister